The Library of Author Biographies™

J. D. Salinger

The Library of Author Biographies™

J. D. SALINGER

Michael A. Sommers

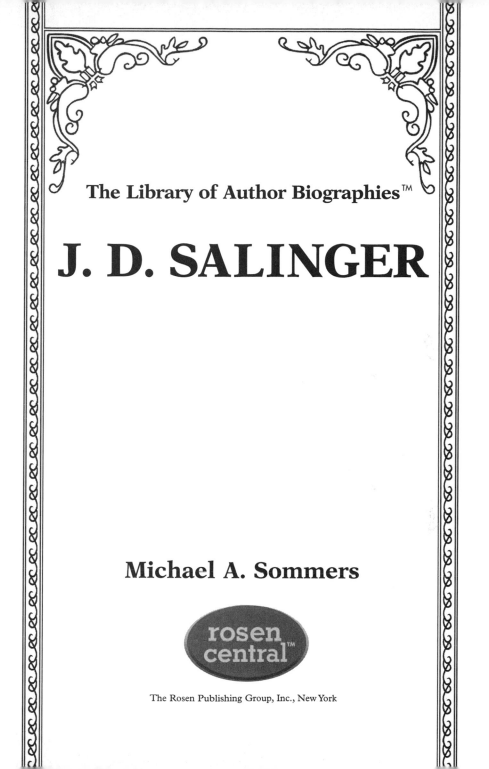

rosen
central™

The Rosen Publishing Group, Inc., New York

To Little Bet

Published in 2006 by The Rosen Publishing Group, Inc.
29 East 21st Street, New York, NY 10010

First Edition

Library of Congress Cataloging-in-Publication Data

Sommers, Michael A.
  J. D. Salinger/Michael A. Sommers.—1st ed.
      p. cm.—(The library of author biographies)
  Includes bibliographical references and index.
  ISBN 1-4042-0460-1 (library binding)
  1. Salinger, J. D. (Jerome David), 1919– 2. Authors, American—20th century—Biography. 3. Salinger, J. D. (Jerome David), 1919– —Interviews. 4. Authors, American—20th century—Interviews.
  I. Title. II. Series.
  PS3537.A426Z885 2006
  813'.54—dc22
                                                          2004026662

Manufactured in the United States of America

By T. Morris Longstreth. Reproduced with permission from the July 19, 1951 issue of *The Christian Science Monitor* (http://www.csmonitor.com/>www.csmonitor.com) © 1951 *The Christian Science Monitor*. All rights reserved.

Reprinted with the permission of Simon & Schuster Adult Publishing Group from *Dream Catcher: A Memoir by Margaret A. Salinger*. Copyright © 2000 by Margaret A. Salinger.

Table of Contents

Introduction: Literature's Most Famous Recluse

Considered one of the most important fiction writers of the twentieth century, J. D. (Jerome David) Salinger is perhaps the most mysterious American author of all time. Tall, handsome, and very charming when he wanted to be, Salinger was always somewhat of a lone wolf. Writing came naturally to him. He started writing fiction when he was eighteen and never stopped.

In his early twenties, Salinger was already publishing critically acclaimed short stories in leading magazines such as *Esquire* and the *New Yorker*. However, nobody, including the author himself, predicted the success of his first (and, to date, his only) novel. Salinger was only thirty-two in 1951 when *The Catcher in the Rye* was published. The thoroughly biting and funny misadventures of a problematic, slang-talking sixteen-year-old boy named Holden Caulfield brought him instant fame. The book was the first twentieth-century novel to deal with the anguish and humor of an adolescent boy in such a realistic fashion. Outspoken, rude, and sometimes very wise, Holden railed against authority figures of every kind in a brash manner seldom before seen in literature.

The story of several intense days in his life touched a nerve with a whole generation of young Americans in their teens and twenties who identified enormously with Holden's rebellious personality. Based on Salinger's own adolescent self, Holden saw much of the world around him as a depressing place populated by fakes and hypocrites whom he referred to as "phonies." Viewed through Holden's eyes, everything from prep schools, churches, and Hollywood movies to parental wisdom, wealth, and success is exposed as phony. This critical attitude disturbed many adults, but endeared him to many young people who were dissatisfied with the conservative America of their parents' generation. The word "phony" became a popular catchphrase for the younger generation.

Meanwhile, critics were impressed with Salinger's colorful language, highly original style, and masterful storytelling skills. *The Catcher in the Rye* went on to become an American classic, read and studied (and sometimes banned) in schools throughout the United States and Canada. Considered one of the forerunners of young adult fiction, it is also routinely heralded as one of the greatest twentieth-century American novels. Although it didn't win any awards in its time, to this day it is routinely included on lists of the most important modern novels and is both admired and studied by scholars all over the world.

The only one who regretted its success was J. D. Salinger himself. Instead of sudden fame and all its trappings, he longed for tranquility and a peaceful place where he could write without journalists, fans, and publishers invading his privacy and bothering him with questions, deadlines, and awards. Disgusted by the world of publishing and celebrity in which he suddenly found himself a sought-after literary star, he escaped to Europe, hoping the fuss would die down. When he returned to the United States and found himself still very much a celebrity, he took drastic steps. He found an isolated cabin, deep in the woods, with beautiful views and no neighbors. It was the perfect refuge. Salinger promptly purchased this patch of wilderness in 1953 and has lived there ever since.

In the isolated hills of New Hampshire, Salinger turned his attention to writing (very long) short stories, all of which focused on the young members of the fictional Glass family. The offspring of two vaudeville entertainers, the Glass children were former child stars, famous for their genius responses on a national radio quiz show. As the charming and slightly crazed young adults of Salinger's stories, the Glasses bickered and inspired each other, had nervous breakdowns, and experienced spiritual awakenings. The two oldest and two youngest of the seven siblings featured prominently in the two last books that Salinger published, *Franny and Zooey* (1961) and *Raise High the Roof Beam, Carpenters and Seymour—an Introduction* (1963). Said a critic at the time, "Rarely if ever in literary history has a handful of stories aroused so much discussion, controversy, praise, denunciation [severe criticism], mystification and interpretation."[1] After provoking so much attention, however, Salinger retreated into silence in 1963.

In the past forty years, J. D. Salinger has not published anything. Perhaps no other living author, let alone one so popular with readers and critics alike, has been surrounded by so much mystery. Salinger, a true recluse, has rarely granted interviews or spoken in public. He guards his privacy so fiercely that over the years, he has been the subject of much curiosity. Among his many fans and admirers, he has gained a cult status as a genius and a rebel. A few literary critics, though, see him as a cranky loner who, with nothing left to write, has remained successful by turning himself into a living mystery. For the most part, however, Salinger is viewed as a talented and brave visionary who is one of the leading literary figures of the late twentieth century.

1 Growing Up

Like his most famous fictional hero, Holden Caulfield, J. D. Salinger has never talked much about his family or his childhood. Even his own children claim he rarely spoke about his years growing up. Perhaps, like Holden, he found "that stuff" boring. What is known about him is that he was born on New Year's Day, 1919, in New York City to Sol and Miriam Salinger.

An Absent Father

Sol Salinger grew up in a religious Jewish family in turn-of-the-century Chicago. When he was twenty-three, Sol took a day trip to a county fair in nearby Ohio. There he met a pretty seventeen-year-old Irish Catholic girl named Marie Jillich, who lived on a nearby farm. Against the wishes of both of their families, the two eloped. In the early twentieth century, marriage between a Jew and a Catholic was often considered unacceptable by members of both religions. Upon marrying Sol, Marie changed her name to Miriam Salinger and never talked to her family again. In keeping with Jewish tradition in which religion is passed down by the mother, Miriam had to be Jewish so that her children would be considered Jews.

In Chicago, Sol ran a movie theater while Miriam took tickets and sold refreshments. During this time, their daughter, Doris, was born. When money got tight, Sol quit and began working for a food importation business that specialized in European meats and cheeses. He did well and was eventually sent to head the company's New York offices. By the time Sonny—the family's nickname for Jerome David—was born in 1919, the Salingers were doing financially well. In 1928, when Sonny was nine, the Salingers moved to an apartment near Central Park on the Upper West Side of Manhattan. Four years later, in the midst of the Great Depression, they moved to a posh Park

Avenue apartment near New York's Metropolitan Museum of Art. During this time, Sonny began attending McBurney School, a private school, in Manhattan.

Salinger was never close to his father, and he has barely ever talked about him. When Sol died in 1970, Salinger didn't even attend the funeral. This absence of a father was later reflected in his fiction. In Salinger's work, fathers are barely seen and rarely spoken of. Salinger's older sister, Doris, however, remembers their father as a kind man who frequently played with them. When, as young children, they went on vacation to the beach, Sol would take them into the ocean and tell them to keep their eyes peeled for "bananafish." This game would later inspire one of Salinger's best-known short stories, "A Perfect Day for Bananafish" (first published in the *New Yorker* in 1948 and later reprinted in *Nine Stories*, 1953), in which Salinger introduced the character of Seymour Glass.

However, Sonny was particularly close to his mother. Therefore, it came as a shock to both Sonny and Doris when they discovered in their teens that Miriam Salinger wasn't really Jewish. Never having converted to Judaism, she was still a Catholic.

Half Jewish

For Salinger, this news was very upsetting. It was difficult because it meant that he was neither Christian nor Jewish. He was without an identity. Because of rising anti-Semitism in the 1930s and 1940s, it was difficult to be fully Jewish, too, but at least Jews had the support and comfort of belonging to a specific religious community. However, growing up, Salinger, like many Jews, suffered from the anti-Semitism that was on the rise in the United States. As a half-Jew coming of age surrounded by Christians, Salinger was particularly sensitive to racial insults.

In Manhattan, the private school Salinger attended was operated by the YMCA (Young Men's Christian Association). The Park Avenue neighborhood where the Salingers lived was largely gentile (non-Jewish). And when, at the age of fifteen, he went away to school at the Valley Forge Military Academy, Salinger no doubt had to deal with anti-Semitism. As his sister, Doris, revealed in a conversation with Salinger's daughter, Margaret, Valley Forge was a tough place for Salinger. These experiences left Salinger very sensitive about his Jewish identity. In her autobiography, *Dream Catcher: A Memoir* (2000),

Rise of Anti-Semitism

The early decades of the twentieth century saw a great increase in immigration to North America. Ten percent of these newcomers to the United States were poor Jews from Eastern Europe, who were the victims of much discrimination. For centuries in Europe, Jews had been persecuted by the Catholic Church and by various rulers, merely for practicing a different religion. In some countries, Jews could only live in certain areas and exercise specific professions. Many Jews left Europe seeking new economic opportunities, as well as religious tolerance. Although things were often better in the New World, Jews were still met with discrimination. Even in New York City, which had a considerably large Jewish population (in the 1920s, 26 percent of the city's population was Jewish), there were many buildings and even neighborhoods with signs in windows reading, "No Jews or dogs allowed." Numerous businesses, both large and small, had a policy of not hiring Jews. Many respected universities such as Harvard and Princeton set limits on the number of Jews who could attend. They believed that too many Jews would make the school unappealing to students from upper-class, gentile families. The Jews who did achieve social and professional success often did so because they didn't "look" or "act" Jewish. Many also changed their names. When he first began sending out short stories, Salinger, who was known by all his friends as "Jerry" (which was often thought of as a Jewish name), carefully signed his name as "J. D."

Salinger's daughter, Margaret, recalls a story he told of his Jewish grandfather coming to visit Manhattan and riding the bus up Madison Avenue with young Salinger. Salinger was terribly embarrassed when his grandfather called out all the street names in a strong Yiddish accent and was met with disapproving glares from the other passengers. However, as a young man, he was also quick to lash out bitterly at the gentile world that discriminated against Jews. Interestingly, like the Salingers, Holden Caulfield and the Glass children also have families in which one parent is Jewish while the other is Irish Catholic. J. D. Salinger has often explained that he writes about "half-Jews" because that's what he knows best.

17

A Very Present Mother

Adolescent Salinger was not altogether unhappy to have to go away to boarding school. He was certainly relieved to get away from home and his parents, particularly his overprotective mother. Although he loved and respected Miriam, he could also become annoyed with her constant fussing over him. In fact, Miriam clearly inspired Bessie, the Irish Catholic mother of the seven Glass siblings, who makes a long and comic appearance in Salinger's story "Zooey" (which first appeared in the *New Yorker* in 1957 before being published in book form in 1961).

In this story, the title character, Zooey Glass, cannot even quietly smoke his cigarette in the bathtub without being interrupted by his mother. Much to his irritation—and despite numerous orders for her to clear out—Bessie perches on the toilet seat and spills out her worries to her handsome actor son. Foremost among them is her concern for her depressed daughter Franny, the youngest Glass sibling and heroine of the story "Franny" (which first appeared in the *New Yorker* in 1955 before being published in book form in 1961).

At Valley Forge, Jerry Salinger began to perfect the art of being a loner. Like Holden Caulfield at his boarding school, Salinger made few close friends. Although attractive and charming, he tended to keep to himself. For the first time, he began to write fiction. He was also literary editor of the yearbook.

When he graduated from high school in 1936, J. D. Salinger had dreams of becoming a professional writer. His practical father felt differently. Since it was the middle of the Depression, Sol wanted his son to secure his future by going to a good university or else joining the family business. However, Jerry had developed a strong hatred for the Ivy League universities (prestigious East Coast universities whose historic buildings were often covered in green ivy), many of which had limits on accepting Jewish students. Like members of his fictional Glass family, he viewed the privileged students and honored professors of distinguished universities such as Princeton as superficial and full of themselves.

Nonetheless, in the fall of 1936, Salinger enrolled at New York University. He lasted only a few months before he dropped out. Unsure of what he wanted to do, he decided to work for his father's import business. In mid-1937, he traveled to Vienna (the capital of Austria) and Poland to learn more about meat and cheeses. In Vienna, he stayed with a Jewish family with whom he became very close. He returned to New York only months before Hitler's Nazis invaded Austria in March 1938. He later discovered that all members of the family he had lived with and grown to love were killed in German concentration camps.

2 Short Stories

B ack in the United States, Salinger decided to give college another try. This time he enrolled at Ursinus College, a small liberal arts college in Pennsylvania. Here, he wrote a column for the campus newspaper. Once again, however, he lasted only a little more than a semester before deciding to drop out.

A First Break

Returning to New York, Salinger decided to seriously try his hand at writing. In the spring of 1939, he began a short-story writing class at Columbia University taught by Whit Burnett, the editor of *Story* magazine. *Story* had published the first works of many young talents who went on to become important American writers, including Norman Mailer (*The Naked and the Dead*, 1948), Tennessee Williams (*The Glass Menagerie*, 1944) and Truman Capote (*Other Voices, Other Rooms*, 1948). Burnett liked Salinger's writing and gave him his first break by publishing his story "The Young Folks" in the March-April 1940 issue of *Story*. Salinger was paid twenty-five dollars for this tale about some wealthy, superficial university students who attend a house party over the holidays. Although not much happens, the story featured elements that would become trademarks of Salinger's fiction: well-drawn adolescent characters, a remarkable ear for lively, realistic teenage slang, and aggressive yet humorous attacks on upper-class, Ivy League–educated phonies.

Only twenty-one years old, Salinger was encouraged by this early success. Before the existence of television, reading was an important form of entertainment for many North Americans. In the 1930s and 1940s, a good number of popular magazines published short fiction. One could actually make a decent living selling short stories to these magazines, which were constantly on the lookout for promising new writers. It would be hard for writers today to imagine earning $27,000 for one short story. However, $27,000 is today's equivalent of the $2,000 that top-selling magazines such as *Collier's*, *Liberty*, *Esquire*, and the *Saturday Evening Post* were paying writers when Salinger started writing. Other good sources of income were women's magazines such as *Lady's Home Journal*, *Good Housekeeping*, *Mademoiselle*, and *Cosmopolitan*, which also published quality fiction. At the time, some stories were so short they could be printed on one page. The fact that people could read them while on the bus or waiting to get a haircut made these stories and the magazines that printed them very popular.

The New Yorker

Meanwhile, Salinger continued to write. Although many of his early manuscripts were rejected, he succeeded in selling three more stories in 1940 and 1941. One appeared in *Collier's* and another in *Esquire*. However, Salinger's big dream was to sell a story to the famous weekly magazine the *New Yorker*. Unlike "slicks," the slang term for thick glossy magazines that were popular but poorly regarded by literary critics, the *New Yorker* was both prestigious and profitable. First published in 1925, the magazine attracted the best writers and paid the highest fees. Since then, the weekly magazine has launched and supported the careers of many of

North America's finest and most celebrated writers. Still being published, it is currently one of the most reputable English-language magazines in the world.

At the end of 1941, it seemed as if Salinger's dream was about to come true. In November, the *New Yorker* accepted a story that he claimed was autobiographical. The story featured an adolescent protagonist by the name of Holden Caulfield. It was the first appearance of the future hero of *The Catcher in the Rye*.

Being published in the *New Yorker* promised to be a major turning point for Salinger's career as a writer. Then, in December 1941, the Japanese bombed Pearl Harbor, in Hawaii, bringing the United States into World War II (1939–1945). This event had several consequences for J. D. Salinger. The first was a delay in the *New Yorker*'s publication of his story (it wouldn't appear until 1946). The second was Salinger's being drafted into the U.S. Army in April 1942. He was twenty-three years old.

Sergeant Salinger

After months of training in the United States, Salinger was promoted to sergeant. Then, in October 1943, he was sent to Maryland to train as a counterintelligence agent. During this time, he continued to write stories and have them published in magazines. These war stories were quite different from his earlier fiction. Instead of dealing with debutantes and prep school boys, the main characters were soldiers being shipped out and the wives and families they left behind. And for the first time ever, his characters—usually lonely outsiders like Salinger himself—had close friends. Indeed, one thing that Salinger himself liked about the army was the friendships he made. As they struggled with the horrors of war, soldiers whose lives were constantly at risk formed extremely close bonds. As John F. "Babe" Gladwaller tells his friend and fellow soldier Vincent Caulfield (the older brother of Holden) in "Last Day of the Last Furlough" (1944), he never knew real friendship until he entered the army.

The character of Babe had much in common with Salinger himself. He was featured in three of the stories that Salinger wrote during the war. Tall and long-legged like Salinger, he also shared the same rank and serial number (ASN 32325200) as his creator. "Last Day of the Last Furlough," the first of the three stories in which Babe appeared, describes him saying good-bye to his family before being shipped out from New York to battle in Europe. In a long-winded, emotional speech that is typical of both Salinger and his characters, he tells his father that war is not like in the movies, but ugly, stupid, and bloody. Afterward, Babe feels embarrassed by his outburst. He seeks out his mother, who is calm and understanding as she deals with her son's departure. Her reaction is nothing like that of Miriam Salinger's real-life reaction to Sonny being shipped off to England in early 1944. To avoid an emotional farewell scene on the docks of New York, Salinger had ordered his mother to stay home. However, as he marched with his battalion toward his ship, he caught sight of Miriam following him, ducking behind lampposts so he wouldn't see her.

Arriving in England, Salinger, along with 800 soldiers, went through a special counterintelligence training course. His time there inspired the first part of the story "For Esmé—with Love and Squalor" (1944). One of his best-known stories (later published in *Nine Stories*), it describes an American soldier meeting with a bright and beautiful young English girl, Esmé. Having finished his training, Sergeant Salinger, like Sergeant X, the hero of "For Esmé," became a special security agent for the Twelfth Infantry Regiment. On June 6, 1944, Salinger and his regiment participated in the famous D-day invasion against German-occupied France. As American, British, and Canadian troops landed on the beaches of Normandy, France, they were attacked by Nazi forces. The horrifying, bloody battle led to the loss of an astounding number of lives, including close to 70 percent of the entire Twelfth Regiment.

The Hardships of War

Once reinforcements arrived to take the place of those who had died, Salinger and the newly re-formed Twelfth Regiment continued on toward Paris. Along the way, they fought, often hand to hand, against German soldiers. Once again, the numbers of dead and wounded on both sides were enormous. Corpses were piled along the roads as the Twelfth Regiment made its way toward the French capital. On August 25, 1944, Salinger was among the first troops to enter Paris, which had recently been liberated from the occupying Nazi forces. During his time in Paris, he took a break from his duties and went to visit the writer Ernest Hemingway, who was working as a war correspondent. The two men got along well. Hemingway had nothing but praise for "Last Day of the Last Furlough," which he had recently read.

Soon after, Salinger and the Twelfth were off to battle again. Winter was approaching as they moved through France and Belgium into Germany. It was freezing cold and wet, and the fields and ditches in which the soldiers dodged bullets and sought shelter were covered with bodies, blood, and icy mud and water. Salinger was eternally grateful to his mother who, every week throughout the war, sent him thick, hand-knit socks. Others were not so lucky; their feet literally froze. A great many soldiers died—from bullet wounds and from freezing to death. Salinger's reactions to these events are simply but strongly described in "A Boy in France" (1945), in which Babe Gladwaller resurfaces on a French battlefield. The chilling narrative details his desperate attempts to sleep in a blood-splattered foxhole that is too short for his long body.

In December, Salinger and the Twelfth helped defend Luxembourg in the famous Battle of the Bulge. So many American soldiers were killed and wounded during this battle that Salinger's family feared him dead. Miraculously, he survived and moved into Germany for the final weeks of fighting before the Germans surrendered and the war was officially declared over on May 8, 1945. As the Allies moved into Germany to try and restore order, counterintelligence agents such as Salinger were kept busy questioning German political prisoners.

Battle Fatigue

Unfortunately, the brutality and hardships of the war had been too much for Salinger. Soon after victory was declared, he was admitted to a German hospital for battle fatigue, today known as post-traumatic stress disorder. Despite this emotional breakdown, Salinger fought being discharged from the army for psychiatric reasons. After a few weeks in the hospital, he was able to persuade the army psychiatrist to let him return to work. However, like the fictional Sergeant X, who is also released from the hospital following a nervous breakdown in the second part of "For Esmé—with Love and Squalor," Salinger was a man who had not survived the war with all his mental faculties intact. Like Sergeant X's, even his handwriting had changed and become almost illegible.

Stationed for six more months in Germany, Salinger met a young woman who had been a low-level official in the Nazi Party. Assigned to arrest and question her, J. D. Salinger also fell in love with her. The woman (named Sylvia) was a beautiful dark-haired doctor with a fiery and independent nature. Before the end of the summer, the two were married. Soon after, they returned to New York. Their married life was intense and passionate, but destructive. Among other things, Sylvia made it clear to Salinger that she hated Jews almost as much as he hated Nazis. Unsurprisingly, their marriage barely lasted more than a few months. Sylvia returned to Europe. In the future, the few times Salinger mentioned her, he referred to her as the evil "Saliva" who had bewitched him.

The Stranger

His intense experiences in the army and war changed Salinger forever. Salinger had been among the first Allied soldiers to enter a German concentration camp and witness firsthand the horrors of the Holocaust. Years later, he claimed he could never completely forget the smell of burning human flesh. Like many soldiers who survived the war, Salinger had difficulty readapting to normal civilian life. In many ways, long after he returned to the United States, he continued to act and react as if a soldier. For example, he kept his hair cut to military regulation and always wore his army watch. He drove a Jeep, crazily, as if he were dodging enemy fire. In the basement of his home, he stored emergency rations of water and other supplies. In her memoir, his daughter, Margaret, complained that when she was a teen, he would interrogate her as if he were still a counterintelligence agent questioning prisoners.

Salinger's feelings about his homecoming are reflected in "The Stranger" (1945), his third and last story to feature Babe Gladwaller. While Babe's friend Vincent Caulfield has been killed in action, Babe returns home, exhausted and feeling like the stranger in the story's title. Babe visits Vincent's girlfriend and tries to explain that Vincent's death wasn't noble like in the movies, but violent and horrible. As he realizes that Vincent's girlfriend, like most American citizens, cannot even imagine what an actual battlefield is like, he becomes confused. He can't decide whether he should tell her the gruesome truth or just clam up and keep his experiences to himself.

Salinger appears to have felt the same way when he returned from the war. Depressed and lonely, he moved out of his parents' home and into a gloomy apartment, where the lack of light, black furniture, and black sheets seemed to match his dark mood. At times, he simply lay on his bed, hardly able to talk or move. During other moments, he was able to write. He set to work on "De Daumier-Smith's Blue Period" (1952), a story about a painter who has just returned from Paris and is having difficulty readjusting to life in New York. What saves Jean de Daumier-Smith from having a nervous breakdown is one of several students who has applied to learn painting from him through a correspondence course. While most of the students are superficial phonies whose dreams of being great artists depress the protagonist, one is a simple nun whose modest paintings strike de Daumier-Smith as pure art. Reading her letters and imagining the nun in her peaceful convent helps de Daumier-Smith to overcome his despair. Coincidentally, shortly after writing this story, a beautiful, innocent girl, fresh out of convent school, would enter Salinger's own life. Her name was Claire, and she would eventually become his second wife.

3 Holden Caulfield

At the same time that he was writing "De Daumier-Smith's Blue Period," J. D. Salinger was also hard at work trying to finish his first and only novel to date. Little did he know that the final published result, entitled *The Catcher in the Rye*, would create an immense literary sensation. Published in 1951, the novel would quickly transform both Salinger and his unforgettable teenage protagonist, Holden Caulfield, into two of the most famous names in twentieth-century literature.

The Catcher in the Rye

It is the late 1940s, just before Christmas, and sixteen-year-old, six-feet-two Holden Caulfield has just been kicked out of Pencey Prep School, an upper-class private boys' school in Pennsylvania. He has failed four out of his five subjects—an avid reader, he does very well in English—and is accused of not "applying himself." This is the latest in a string of fancy private schools from which Holden has been expelled. Because of this, he is in no hurry to return to his wealthy Manhattan home and face his parents. Neither does he want to stick around his dreary boarding school whose professors and students he views as shallow.

He decides to take what money he has and spend some time on his own in New York. Checking into a seedy hotel, he passes the next few days in a series of strange misadventures that involve a colorful collection of characters including taxi drivers, three girls from Seattle, two nuns, an elevator man, a prostitute, and an old girlfriend with whom he tries to elope. During this time, he visits nightclubs and bars, gets drunk and tries to have sex, goes skating and to the theater, walks aimlessly for blocks, and sleeps in Grand Central Station in New York City. Each of these episodes leaves him feeling increasingly lonely and depressed about people in general and the world at large.

Finally, in despair, he sneaks into his parents' apartment and wakes up his beloved ten-year-old sister, Phoebe. After she scolds him for not just hating school, but hating everybody, Holden is moved to tears. He breaks down and confesses what he'd really like to be: a catcher in the rye.

He tells Phoebe how he often imagines thousands of little kids playing in a field of rye. And he, Holden, is the only older person around. At the edge of the field is a great cliff, and it is up to Holden to catch the children if they run too close to the edge and risk falling off. This is what he would love to do all day—be a "catcher" in the rye.

Soon after confessing his dream to Phoebe, he hears his parents returning home. Holden sneaks out and seeks refuge with a former teacher, who tells him that he is going to have serious problems if he doesn't change his attitude. Holden falls asleep and wakes up to discover his teacher stroking his head. Confused and disgusted, he flees. He decides that he wants to run away to the West Coast and start a new life where nobody knows him. However, before he does this, Holden wants to see Phoebe one last time. The two meet in front of the Metropolitan Museum of Art, where Phoebe announces that she plans to accompany Holden. When he objects, Phoebe turns her back on him. This act startles Holden, since Phoebe is one of the only people he truly loves. To patch things up, he takes Phoebe to the carousel at Central Park and, after promising to return home with her, buys her as many rides as she wants. Watching Phoebe, for the first time Holden feels so happy that he is close to crying.

The novel ends with Holden returning home, physically and mentally ill. He is sent to a psychiatric clinic, somewhere in California where a lot of people, particularly one psychoanalyst, keep asking him if he's going to "apply himself" when he gets out and returns to school. Holden expresses typical teenage frustration at the "stupid" question. After all, he argues, how does anyone know what they are going to do until they actually go and do it?

A Great, Controversial Novel

The Catcher in the Rye was very different from any other American novel that had been published. Salinger himself said he had written the book for young people. However, it was the first time that a novel for teenagers was actually written in the first person using the raw, slangy, and even rude language of a contemporary American sixteen-year-old male. The novel was also bold in its treatment of certain taboo subjects that had not yet been discussed in books for young people. It followed its underage hero as he challenged authority, told lies, got rip-roaring drunk, and had an experience with a prostitute. Along the way, it criticized many elements of a conventional, middle-class American way of life—which shocked and outraged some readers.

Before *The Catcher in the Rye*, the few novels written specifically for young people had mostly been moral stories, full of lessons about growing up to become good, successful young men or women. They were generally concerned with improving young people's minds and setting good examples of proper behavior. *The Catcher in the Rye* shattered this tradition and, in doing so, paved the way for the realistic and complex young adult fiction that began emerging in the late 1960s and early 1970s.

This slim novel, fewer than 200 pages long, generated an enormous amount of discussion. Overall, people either loved it or hated it. Some considered it to be a work of genius and a great American coming-of-age novel, in the tradition of Mark Twain's great nineteenth-century classic *Huckleberry Finn* (1885). Other readers viewed it as offensive, disgusting, and even dangerous trash.

What the Critics Said About *The Catcher in the Rye*

"Profoundly moving and a disturbing book, but it is not hopeless."[1] —*Saturday Review of Literature*

"Not fit for children to read."[2] —*Christian Science Monitor*

"He [Salinger] can understand an adolescent mind without displaying one."[3]—*Time*

"An unusually brilliant novel."[4] —*New York Times*

"A brilliant tour-de-force, but in a writer of Salinger's undeniable talent one expects something more."[5] —*New Republic*

"[Salinger] knows how to write about kids. This book, though, it's too long. Gets kind of monotonous. And he should have cut out a lot about these jerks and all at that crumby school. They depress me. They really do."[6] —*New York Times*

Many critics, such as those writing for the *New Yorker,* the *New York Times,* and the *New Republic*, thought that Salinger's novel was nothing less than brilliant. They applauded the vibrant first-person narrative. They praised Holden's—and Salinger's—descriptions and opinions as a sensitive and truthful critique of contemporary American life with its many failings and hypocrisies. To many of these critics, *The Catcher in the Rye* was an example of great American literature.

However, other critics were clearly unimpressed with the book. There were those—such as *New York Times* critic James Stern, who wrote a review in language imitating Holden Caulfield (see final review, page 38)—who found the novel to be rambling, repetitive, and filled with too many depressing scenes and characters. Some reviewers and readers found Holden's ranting and observations—endlessly sprinkled with "depressing" and "phony"—to be boring to the point of irritation. Others were frankly shocked by the use of four-letter words. They felt this "dirty" novel needed to be banned from bookstore and library shelves. It should definitely not be read, let alone taught, in schools.

From the beginning, there was a reaction to ban the novel from schools. In fact, between 1966 and 1975, *The Catcher in the Rye* was the most frequently banned book in American schools. This censorship battle is still being waged today. Currently, Salinger's novel is on the reading lists of many public schools throughout the United States and Canada. It also remains one of the books most challenged by concerned parents who object to its sexual content, rough language, and lack of morality.

An Unforgettable Antihero

Salinger's writing talent aside, what made (and continues to make) *The Catcher in the Rye* so popular and original is its main character and narrator, Holden Caulfield. As both a memorable literary character and a complex portrait of a contemporary North American adolescent, Holden has left an indelible mark on world literature. Part of this success is due to his realistic, terribly human personality, with all its good points, flaws, inconsistencies, and conflicts. As such, he is the perfect example of a modern literary antihero, a complex hero whose essential goodness coexists with negative traits traditionally associated with villains.

Highly intelligent, Holden is a perpetual dropout who won't "apply himself." He has strong opinions on almost every subject, and he airs them nonstop. Yet, like any teenager, he is plagued by doubts and insecurities. A restless adventurer and risk-taker, he is also a self-confessed coward. Although he toughly (and stupidly) stands up to a burly brute of an elevator operator who insists upon receiving $5, he is sensitive and emotional, breaking into sobs in front of his ten-year-old sister, Phoebe. Desperate loneliness causes him to constantly seek out the company of others. Yet he is also a social rebel who can't stand the fakeness and conformity of cliques and groups—whether they be the supporters of his high school football team or wealthy New York socialites such as his parents and girlfriend. His dream is to run away out West, where he can live as a deaf-mute so that he won't ever have to make conversation with another living soul.

Many adult readers had a profound dislike of Holden Caulfield. Some members of the Christian Church and quite a few parents objected to Holden's rude language and lack of morals. They viewed him as a pervert, a psychopath, and a dangerous influence on young readers. They were shocked by his irresponsibility and antiauthoritarian stance. Despite his obvious intelligence, he chose to be a failure. Instead of being a team player surrounded by friends, he chose to love only his dead brother and kid sister. Instead of being a strong leader, he withdrew from society, whereupon he suffered a mental breakdown. More an antihero than a hero, he was definitely

What the Critics Said About Holden Caulfield

"A lanky, crew-cut 16, well-born Holden Caulfield is sure all the world is out of step but him. His code is the survival of the flippest, and he talks a lingo as forthright and gamy in its way, as a soldier's."[7]—*Time*

"Holden, who is the clown, villain, and even moderately, the hero of this tale . . . is so super-sensitive to others' faults that he has no friends, among boys at least. He is as unbalanced as a rooster on a tightrope . . . He is alive, human, preposterous, profane and pathetic beyond belief."[8]—*Christian Science Monitor*

"What was wrong with Holden was his moral revulsion against anything that was ugly, evil, cruel, or what he called 'phoney' and his acute responsiveness to beauty and innocence, especially the innocence of the very young, in whom he saw reflected his own lost childhood . . . An unusually sensitive and intelligent boy."[9]—*Saturday Review of Literature*

"Holden is bewildered, lonely, ludicrous and pitiful. His troubles, his failings are not of his own making but of a world that is out of joint. There is nothing wrong with him that a little understanding and affection, preferably from his parents, couldn't have set right. Though confused and unsure of himself, like most 16-year-olds, he is observant and perceptive and filled with a certain wisdom. His minor delinquencies seem minor indeed when contrasted with adult delinquencies with which he is confronted."[10]—*New York Times*

"A sad, screwed-up guy,"[11]—Charles Kegel, "Incommunicability in Salinger's *The Catcher in the Rye*"

young man whom one would call a good influence. This view was summed up in a review published in the *Christian Science Monitor*. Founded by members of the Christian Science Church, this widely read national newspaper noted, "Fortunately, there cannot be many of him [Holden] yet. But one fears that a book like this given wide circulation may multiply his kind—as too easily happens when immorality and perversion are recounted by writers of talent . . . "[12]

Of course, it was precisely this refreshing blast of realism, with all of its messy problems, heart-tugging emotions, and human imperfections that made Holden Caulfield so popular with so many readers, especially young ones. Sarcastic and scared, charming and annoying, Holden was a contemporary with whom young people could identify. Furthermore, in the years following World War II, many young soldiers, like Salinger himself, had returned from the war to an America that didn't recognize their efforts. They felt as left out and alienated from American society as Holden Caulfield did. Accordingly, they began to question many accepted notions about an American way of life. So did many students at schools and universities across the nation, who were coming of age. With the end of the war, although America was economically booming, some young people felt that there was something missing in their lives. Unlike their parents, they felt there might be more to life than prosperity and success. As a rebel against a safe and wealthy society full of rigid rules and false appearances, Holden was a very appealing character.

He was also a symbol of the future. His anti-authority stance would become a permanent part of American youth culture that would evolve throughout the second half of the twentieth century. On the tail of Holden Caulfield came Marlon Brando (*The Wild One*, 1953) and James Dean (*Rebel Without a Cause*, 1956). These two important movie stars enjoyed immense popularity in the early 1950s. They played attractive and dangerous young rebels on screen and in the public eye. Their rebellious attitudes prefigured the birth of rock music in the 1950s, with the rise of young stars like Elvis Presley and, later, the Beatles and the Rolling Stones—all of whom were worshiped by youths while initially disapproved of by many of their parents.

The ideals Holden expressed and came to symbolize also echoed those embraced during the massive student protests (for civil rights, and against the Vietnam War) of the 1960s and early 1970s. Holden Caulfield would have been thrilled to witness students across America taking to the streets and university campuses to protest government actions and to speak out against the conformist rules laid down by their parents, school administrators, church officials, and lawmakers. It is for this challenging of authority—so important in youth culture—that Holden Caulfield is still so popular with young people. Today, his expressions might seem a bit dated, but his personality and ideals continue to affect readers who still buy hundreds of thousands of copies of the classic novel every year.

4 The Glass Family

Shortly before *The Catcher in the Rye* was released, J. D. Salinger made his publisher, Little, Brown & Company, promise not to send him any reviews of the novel. As well, he was not at all pleased that a close-up photo of him had been printed on the book's jacket. He was so horrified to see the image of his face magnified that he asked the publisher to remove it from future editions of the book. In fact, he would eventually request that photos never accompany his published work.

Nobody, including Salinger himself, ever imagined that *The Catcher in the Rye* would experience such tremendous success. It remained on the *New York Times*'s bestseller list for twenty-nine weeks. Subsequently, it was translated into more than fifteen languages. Also, it was chosen by the library staff of the United States Information Service as one of the twelve best American novels published after World War II. Among these books—which included works by Norman Mailer, Philip Roth, Jack Kerouac, and John Updike—the report stated that "it soon became first favorite among students in the Western world."[1]

A Little Cabin

Unsurprisingly, the author (always a very private person) was not at all prepared for the fame that followed. To avoid fans, he escaped to Europe, but when he returned to the United States the attention still hadn't died down. While working on *Catcher*, Salinger had often referred to it as an autobiographical novel. Now, unhappy with all the attention he was getting, Salinger decided to follow the lead of Holden Caulfield, who longed to run away to a place where nobody knew him.

In *Catcher*, Holden dreamed of retreating to the woods where he would build a little cabin. He would meet and marry a beautiful girl, and the two would live together in the woods for the rest of their lives. If his wife wanted to talk to him, she—like everybody else—would have to write Holden a note. And if they decided to have children, they would hide them away from the world. He and his wife would purchase books for the children and teach them to read and write at home.

Unlike Holden's dream, that of Salinger became reality. Feeling imprisoned by his fame, Salinger decided to buy a cabin in the woods with the money he had made from his novel. He found the perfect place in the isolated hills of New Hampshire, near the village of Cornish. It was a small, rotting, wooden house that was painted red. It offered magnificent views of woods, meadows, and the distant Adirondack Mountains. Even though the house was in terrible shape, Salinger decided it was perfect and he bought it. Here he would be able to focus on his life's work—his writing—without any interruptions. He moved into the Red House, as he called it, on New Year's Day of 1953, the day he turned thirty-four.

"This Beautiful Girl"

By now Salinger also had the beautiful girl. He had met one in 1950, at a party in New York. Claire Douglas was a shy and stunning sixteen-year-old. She had just left her convent school because she hadn't wanted to become a nun. Instead, she was finishing her senior year of high school at Shipley, a private boarding school for girls. Although Claire was half his age, thirty-one-year-old Salinger was very struck with her. He even modeled Jane Gallagher, the girl whom Holden Caulfield worships in *The Catcher in the Rye* (and who also attends Shipley) after Claire.

Over the next year, Salinger frequently wrote and phoned Claire at her private school. During weekends and vacations, they spent a fair amount of time together. Claire was terribly in awe of Salinger, who was extremely intelligent and charming. When Salinger moved to New Hampshire, Claire was enrolled at nearby Radcliffe College, in Cambridge, Massachusetts. She often came to spend weekends with him in the country. At one point, Salinger asked Claire to drop out of college and move in with him. When she refused, he disappeared.

Ultimately, Claire was so desperate without Salinger, she suffered from a nervous breakdown and ended up marrying a banker, whom she didn't love. A few months later, she was divorced. Then, in the summer of 1954, Salinger reappeared. Overjoyed, she quickly moved in with him. Each week, they would leave Cornish and drive down to Cambridge. While Claire lived in a house with other young women and attended classes at Radcliffe, Salinger stayed in a hotel and tried to work on a new story he was writing. Since *The Catcher in the Rye*, he had published three short stories, two of them in the *New Yorker* (with which he would continue to publish exclusively). In 1953, nine of his best short stories were selected for publication in book form by Little, Brown & Company under the title *Nine Stories*.

Salinger complained that all the driving from Cornish to Cambridge and back was making it difficult for him to complete his new story. "Franny" was finally published in the *New Yorker* in January 1955. That same month, Salinger gave Claire another choice to make: drop out of college and elope with him or their relationship would be over for good. Only four months remained before Claire would receive her university degree. However, she still remembered with horror the last time she had rejected Salinger's marriage proposal. In February, she left Radcliffe. That same month, the two were married by a justice of the peace in Vermont.

"Franny"

In Margaret Salinger's memoir, *Dream Catcher*, Claire recounts that the thirty-seven-page story that Salinger called "Franny" was actually all about her. Claire was the inspiration for the beautiful college student who arrives to spend the weekend with her handsome but superficial Ivy League boyfriend Lane, only to experience the beginnings of a nervous breakdown. Franny's despair is caused by what she views as the meaningless world of parties, football games, and academic posturing that surrounds her. Seeking escape from her reality, she turns to a slim, green book called *The Way of a Pilgrim*. The book contains a prayer to Jesus that Franny has been quietly chanting under her breath until it becomes as natural to her as breathing. She hopes, in this way, to receive the spiritual enlightenment the book promises. While at Radcliffe, Claire experienced a similar spiritual and emotional crisis. For a while she, like Franny, sought relief in *The Way of a Pilgrim*. She hoped that muttering the Jesus prayer over and over again would give her some peace of mind.

"Franny" was the first story Salinger had published in two years. By the time he sat down to write it, he was searching for new answers to his own spiritual crisis, which had been building up ever since he returned to America after the war. In the late 1940s, while he was still living in New

York, he had become interested in Eastern religion and philosophy, particularly the teachings of Zen Buddhism. Salinger read many books about Buddhism and meditated a lot. For a while, he seriously considered retreating from the world and becoming a monk. Then, in the early 1950s, he began studying a form of Hinduism—Vedanta—with a swami, or Hindu religious leader, in New York City. According to Vedanta teachings, a man in search of spiritual peace and enlightenment had to show great self-discipline. This included giving up women and "gold," or material objects, both of which are considered obstacles to spiritual purity.

The influences of these Eastern philosophies contributed to Salinger's desire to remove himself from New York and what he viewed as the superficial aspects of fame, such as giving interviews, being photographed, and receiving awards and honors. They also explain his early relationship with Claire, a seemingly innocent girl, for whom—in keeping with Vedantic views on marriage—he was more of a teacher than a lover. These new religious explorations also spilled over into the short stories Salinger wrote following *The Catcher in the Rye*. They were somewhat present in "De Daumier-Smith's Blue Period." They were even more pronounced in "Teddy" (1953), the last story included in *Nine Stories*.

At first, the title character appears to be a normal, if exceptionally bright, little boy with dirty sneakers, a ratty T-shirt, and hair that needs cutting. As the story begins, he is traveling aboard a luxury cruise ship in the company of his wealthy parents and sister. However, it turns out that Teddy is not just an average American boy on vacation, but a philosopher and a visionary who has puzzled the Ivy League professors who line up to interview him. Teddy is capable of seeing into the future and can even predict his own death. He also believes in the Vedantic view of reincarnation, or rebirth. For this reason, he is completely unafraid to die.

Children: Fictional and Real

Following publication of *The Catcher in the Rye*, Salinger declared in interviews that, like Holden Caulfield, he too was fascinated with the innocence and purity of children. "Some of my best friends are children," he told *Time* magazine in 1951. "In fact, all of my best friends are children."[2] He made a similar statement to the *Christian Science Monitor*, where, in response to some adults' desire to censor *The Catcher in the Rye*, he expressed his disappointment at the thought that his book would be kept out of young people's reach.

Indeed, when he first moved to New Hampshire, before marrying, he became close friends with some local high school students, one of whom later described him as just like one of the gang. He loved the company of young people and often threw parties at the Red House. Claire, too, was childlike in age and innocence. In fact, she claims that her marriage to Salinger started to have serious problems when she became pregnant. As her belly grew bigger and bigger, Salinger became increasingly horrified. Forced to face that Claire was a full-fledged woman and not a "nice," pure, innocent girl like Franny, Phoebe Caulfield, or young Esmé from "To Esmé—with Love and Squalor," he began to distance himself from her.

When twenty-two-year-old Claire gave birth to a baby girl in December 1955, Salinger was initially delighted to have a child in his home. Although Salinger had wanted to name her Phoebe after Holden Caulfield's little sister, Claire insisted that her daughter have her own name— Margaret Ann. Salinger was equally pleased, when five years later, in 1960, Claire gave birth to a son, Matthew. When he wasn't busy writing, Salinger loved to spend time with both of his children. In her autobiography, Margaret Salinger recalls that unlike most other parents who treated their offspring like kids, Salinger always treated his son and daughter like adults. When they were children and, later, teenagers, he never talked down to them, and always respected their opinions.

However, as a full-time author who was obsessed with his writing, Salinger found himself unprepared to deal with the real-life demands of being a father. During Margaret's first month of life, Salinger was driven so crazy by her frequent crying that he immediately began construction of a one-room cabin far off in the forest, where he could write in peace. At this point in his career, Salinger was sometimes writing up to sixteen hours a day. He often stayed up all night and into the next day.

In November 1955, the *New Yorker* had published another long story of his, "Raise High the Roof Beam, Carpenters," in which Salinger introduced the character of Buddy Glass (brother of Franny), Boo Boo ("Down at the Dinghy"), and Seymour ("A Perfect Day for Bananafish"). Meanwhile, he was hard at work on his next story about yet another member of the Glass family.

When he wasn't busy writing, however, Salinger adored spending time with his daughter.

In her, he saw all the imagination, potential, and lack of phoniness that disgusted him in the hypocritical adult world beyond the forest with its emphasis on wealth, fame, and conformity. While he treated her like a fairy princess, he remained more and more distant from Claire, who grew increasingly depressed and lonely. When she left school to marry him, Salinger had discouraged her from maintaining relationships with her family and friends and her professors at Radcliffe. He

The Green House

Salinger's new writing studio was built out of concrete blocks. Because they were painted dark green, he called it the Green House. Inside, against one wall, there was a cot where Salinger could sleep. Against the opposite wall was his desk and chair. His desk was a plain slab of wood upon which sat his manual typewriter. His chair was a brown leather car seat, large enough for him to sit on in the cross-legged lotus position (a yoga pose) and meditate. The walls were covered with Post-It–like slips of paper with notes. When a fire damaged the Green House in 1992, Salinger rescued the chair and the typewriter, which he still uses.

didn't want any elements of the real, outside world disturbing the perfect life he was trying to create in the woods. By the time of Margaret's birth, weeks would pass without a human being visiting the Salingers' house. It was also very rare for Claire and Margaret to leave the Red House in the woods.

During the winter of 1957, Claire was on the verge of another nervous breakdown. Terribly unhappy, she left Salinger. Taking Margaret, she went to stay with her family in New York City, where she began seeing a psychiatrist three times a week. Four months later, Salinger arrived on Claire's doorstep and persuaded her to return home. She did so only after he agreed to let both Margaret and herself have some friends. Around that time, in May, the *New Yorker* published the story Salinger had been working on for the last two years: "Zooey."

The House of Glass

"Zooey" picked up where "Franny" left off. In fact, the two stories were published together as a book in 1961. "Zooey" takes place in the messy Manhattan apartment of the Glass family, where Franny has collapsed after the nervous breakdown referred to in "Franny." Apart from long conversations, not much happens in this very long short story, which takes place over a few hours. An anguished Franny cries, stares into space, and refuses the chicken soup offered by her worried mother, Bessie. Meanwhile, egged on by Bessie, her older brother, Zooey, tries to convince Franny that her obsession with the Jesus prayer contained in *The Way of the Pilgrim* is as selfish and superficial as the world that so disgusts her.

The characters of Franny, Zooey, and Bessie are rich and complex—and in Bessie's case, often quite humorous. However, as many critics pointed out, most of this story consists of the often excessive ramblings of its title character with respect to religious and philosophical questions. Writing in the *New York Times*, noted author John Updike praised Salinger for "risk[ing] such a wealth of words upon events that are purely internal and deeds that are purely talk."[3] At the same time, Updike accused Salinger of loving his characters too much. As he puts it, "'Zooey' is just too long; there are too many cigarettes, too many ——s . . . "[4]

As a character, Zooey bears certain similarities to both Holden Caulfield and J. D. Salinger himself. Intelligent and sarcastic, Zooey is also a loner who has trouble connecting with people. When he criticizes Franny for retreating from the world, she later shoots back his own criticism at him by pointing out that the only people he ever wants to meet for a drink are either dead or not available. Zooey's antisocial nature is also a characteristic shared by the two oldest Glass brothers, Seymour and Buddy, both of whom make appearances in the story. The narrator and supposed author of "Zooey," Buddy Glass, is a Salinger-like, middle-aged writer and English professor at a private school for girls. He lives alone in a modest cabin in the New England woods, where—much to the despair of Bessie, who can never get in touch with him—he has no close neighbors and not even a telephone.

Buddy first appeared as the supposed author and narrator of an earlier story, "Raise High the Roof Beams, Carpenters," which first appeared in the *New Yorker* in 1955, before being published in book form in 1963. This highly comic tale introduces Buddy, who is a World War II soldier. On leave from the army, Buddy travels to New York for the wedding of his older brother, Seymour, to a beautiful high-society girl named Muriel. The only member of the Glass family to attend Seymour's wedding, Buddy feels out of place among Muriel's numerous friends and family members, whom he perceives as shallow socialites dripping with money and exhibiting bad taste. However, he feels even worse when Seymour—whom Muriel's family already considers crazy and unstable—fails to show up at the church for his own wedding.

Amid much outrage, the marriage is called off. Upon leaving the church, Buddy ends up in a car with furious members of Muriel's wedding party. When they discover that he is Seymour's brother, Muriel's friends lash out at him, calling Seymour all sorts of names. Yet, when their cab gets stuck in traffic in terrible summer heat, they find themselves unable to refuse Buddy's invitation for a cold drink at the Glass brothers' apartment, which is conveniently located nearby. While the members of the wedding party get drunk, Buddy wanders off. He stumbles across Seymour's diary and goes into the bathroom to read it. In his diary (reprinted word for word in the story), Seymour confesses his love for Muriel, whose beautiful simplicity and honesty he worships. He also expresses his desire to elope with her instead of participating in a big wedding. Like Salinger himself, Seymour admits to reading much Eastern and Vedantic theory, which views marriage as a rite in which husband and wife inspire, teach, and serve each other.

John Updike called "Raise High the Roof Beams, Carpenters" the best of all of Salinger's stories about the Glass family. As he stated, it's "a magic and hilarious prose-poem."[5] Many critics have agreed. They, and countless readers, certainly found it much easier going than "Zooey" or Salinger's next published piece, "Seymour—an Introduction" (first published in the *New Yorker* in 1959 and in book form in 1963). This last work, also written and narrated by Buddy Glass is, as critic Warren French has pointed out in *J. D. Salinger: Revisited* (1988), a critical study of the author—much more of a long composition than a story.

In more than 100 fascinating, but often unbearably dense and repetitive pages, Buddy attempts to pin down in words the brilliant poet, crazy genius, and visionary saint who was his older brother, Seymour. The eldest Glass was a hero to all the younger Glass children. The story leads him from Seymour's childhood success as a whiz kid on a radio show quiz game up to his marriage to Muriel, which ends when he kills himself on his honeymoon (recounted in "A Perfect Day for Bananafish"). Aside from these biographical details, Buddy devotes numerous pages to reproducing Seymour's Japanese haikus (traditional three-line Japanese poems) and describing his fantastic technique for playing marbles. As John

Updike has pointed out, the problem with "Seymour" is that instead of writing about a genius, Buddy and J. D. Salinger are lecturing about one. The results are, in the words of another critic, "intolerably [extremely] dull . . . lacking the charm, humor and surface brilliance which distinguish most of Mr. Salinger's stories."[6]

5 Silence

To many, "Seymour—an Introduction," which was published in book form together with "Raise High the Roof Beam, Carpenters" in 1963, seemed to confirm that Salinger was in danger of becoming overly caught up in, and perhaps obsessed with, his own material. Two years later, he published the story "Hapworth 16, 1924" in the *New Yorker*. The character of Buddy Glass introduces the story, which takes the form of a very long letter Seymour had written to his family from Hapworth summer camp. Although Seymour was supposedly seven years old at the time, the letter is written in an extremely articulate adult-like voice. In it, Seymour complains about being sent away to camp and lectures his parents and all of his siblings on various matters. He then discusses at great length his strong views about writing and writers in a preachy style that much of the reading public, including most literary critics, found unreadable.

Noted author and critic Mary McCarthy responded to "Seymour—an Introduction" with the comment, "Salinger's world contains nothing but Salinger."[1] Meanwhile, even longtime fans of the Glass family stories (who in 1961 had kept *Franny and Zooey* on the *New York Times*'s best-seller list for more than six months), found "Seymour" and "Hapworth" quite unbearable. The author John Updike accused Salinger of coming to love the Glass family, and particularly Seymour, the family genius, with so much intensity that he could no longer see them as characters. He argued that the Glass family had become a refuge for Salinger, an observation backed up by Salinger's daughter, Margaret. In her memoir, she often refers to Buddy and Seymour as "fictional siblings" with whom she competed for her father's attention and affection. She points out that her father seemed to love the company of his invented characters more than that of the majority of living human beings, most of whom he, like Holden

Caulfield, Zooey, Buddy, and Seymour Glass, viewed as "phonies."

Whether or not Salinger agreed with his critics and readers, nobody knows. "Hapworth 16, 1924" would be the last Glass story, or any piece of writing for that matter, that Salinger would ever publish. Salinger might have been unhappy with his last Glass installment since he didn't seek to publish the story in book form. In the late 1990s, amid great expectations, rumors circulated that the small independent Orchises Press was set to publish "Hapworth." So far, however, this has not occurred.

Some critics have proposed that after "Hapworth," Salinger lost his nerve as a writer. In *J. D. Salinger: Revisited*, author Warren French suggests that as the years went by, Salinger's escape to the New Hampshire woods isolated him from the world at large and from his readers. *The Catcher in the Rye* had struck a chord with an entire generation of young people because of its intensely vibrant protagonist who spoke in everyday language about very modern concerns such as sexuality, depression, loneliness, and conformity. Meanwhile, "Seymour" and "Hapworth" featured an almost inhuman artist-visionary whose rambling, self-centered lectures about spiritual matters were almost impossible for American readers of any age to identify with, let alone read.

A Recluse

Salinger never liked publishing or its rewards. "It's a —— embarrassment publishing," he once said to a fellow writer. "The poor boob who lets himself in for it might as well walk down Madison Avenue with his pants down."[2] Since he stopped publishing, J. D. Salinger has continued to live the life of a recluse in the woods. For money, he lives off the royalties from sales of his books. To this day, approximately 300,000 copies of *The Catcher in the Rye* alone are sold every year, making it one of the best-selling American novels of all time. Although, as far as the public knows, he has produced no new fiction in close to forty years, Salinger's mysterious lifestyle has made him a fascinating figure. In a sense, his isolation has only increased curiosity about him and added to his fame. Old fans and new readers return time and time again to his four published books (particularly *The Catcher in the Rye*) hoping to find a further glimpse into his private life.

In 1967, Salinger and Claire were divorced. For years, they had been living in separate houses in the woods, often not seeing each other for days on end. Margaret and Matthew spent most of their time with their mother. Later on, like Holden Caulfield, they were sent away to private boarding schools. They only saw their father during holidays and often for only short periods of time. Salinger couldn't stand anything or anyone distracting him from his writing.

According to the very few interviews he has given, Salinger does continue to write. However, instead of writing for the world at large, he writes for himself. In *Dream Catcher*, Margaret Salinger recalls an occasion when her father told a friend that for him the act of writing was part of a search for spiritual enlightenment. He intended to devote himself to one great work of writing and that work would be his life. Anything from the real world— publishers, the press, friends, even family members—that got in the way of his work, causing him to interrupt his quest, became obstacles from which he had to distance himself.

Throughout the years, Salinger has also looked for spiritual enlightenment in other ways. Aside from exploring Zen Buddhism and Vedanta Hinduism, he also immersed himself in Christian Science and Scientology. He wholeheartedly embraced many of these belief systems, only to reject them months or years later when they failed to bring him the peace of mind he sought. Similarly, over the years he has practiced yoga and meditation, macrobiotics, homeopathy, and acupuncture.

Margaret Salinger recalls that during her childhood, her father would often work obsessively on a piece of writing. Frustrated at not being able to finish it, he would then disappear, often for weeks. Usually, he would go to another city, check into a hotel, and not see or talk to anybody. When Salinger finally returned home, he would often have completely destroyed whatever he was writing. Meanwhile, he had often discovered a new religion or philosophy, the rules of which he, his wife, and his children would now be expected to follow.

Ultimately, Salinger sought spiritual salvation in the stories he wrote. In the company of his beloved fictional characters (all of whom were depressed by the materialistic, meaningless world that surrounded them) he went looking for spiritual answers to the world's confusion. In his early writings, his characters—most of whom, like Babe Gladwaller, Sergeant X, and Holden Caulfield, had many aspects in common with Salinger himself— were saved by "nice," pure, innocent children. Mattie (Babe's ten-year-old sister), Esmé (the beautiful young English girl who writes letters to

Sergeant X following his nervous breakdown), and Phoebe Caulfield are the bright and promising young girls who save Salinger's male protagonists from despair and loneliness and provide them with hope. This was a pattern Salinger would also repeat in his own life. After Claire, he had several relationships with innocent, beautiful women who were much younger than himself. One such woman, a tiny red-haired girl named Colleen (Gaelic for "young girl"), became Salinger's third wife when he was well into his seventies. Another girl with whom Salinger was involved, Joyce Maynard, went on to become an important author. In 1998, Maynard published a memoir entitled *At Home in the World*. In its pages, for the first time, she decided to break the silence surrounding her nine-month relationship with J. D. Salinger.

In the nearly four decades since Salinger last published, Maynard's memoir is one of the few instances in which new information about the writer has come to the public's attention. The residents of Cornish, where Salinger lives, are incredibly protective of their famous neighbor's privacy. They refuse to give details about his life to snooping journalists or fans. Those who have not respected his privacy have met with quick retaliation. For example, in 1974, a pirated edition of Salinger's *Complete*

Uncollected Short Stories was published by an unknown source in California. The two-volume collection surfaced in San Francisco and rapidly sold out in the city's bookshops. However, Salinger quickly got wind of this unauthorized collection and immediately sought justice. Outraged, he also spoke to a reporter for the first time in more than twenty years. In an interview with the *New York Times*, he talked about his privacy and his desire to write in peace, for his own pleasure.

It wasn't until 1986 that the legal suit Salinger brought against San Francisco bookstores that sold his *Complete Uncollected Short Stories* was finally settled in the author's favor. That same year, Salinger once again went to court—this time to fight the publication of a biography about him. Without seeking his permission, British writer Ian Hamilton had written *J. D. Salinger: A Writing Life*. Salinger was furious, claiming that reproducing his private letters while he was still alive was a copyright infringement. He tried to ban the book's publication on the grounds that Hamilton quoted from his personal letters. The dispute went all the way to the U.S. Supreme Court, which, in 1987, ruled in favor of Salinger. Hamilton had to rewrite a significant amount of his book. It was finally released in 1988 under the title *In Search of J. D. Salinger.*

Joyce Maynard

It was 1972 and Joyce Maynard was an eighteen-year-old freshman at Yale University who had just published an essay in the *New York Times Magazine*. Entitled "An 18-Year-Old Looks Back on Life," the essay was an autobiographical account of Maynard's teenage life. Young adult readers identified with her story so much that she became famous overnight. The fact that the magazine's cover featured an attractive photo of this striking young woman didn't hurt her popularity. Maynard received a great many fan letters. One of the most charming was from fifty-three-year-old J. D. Salinger. The two spent several weeks writing to each other. When they finally met, Maynard instantly fell in love with the reclusive legend. Struck by her beauty and talent, Salinger persuaded her to drop out of school. In turn, she was impressed by his charm and intelligence. Turning her back on her friends, family, and the hounding press and public, Maynard moved in with Salinger.

Their relationship lasted nine months. Salinger was irritated by Maynard's sloppy habits and the fact that she only read *TV Guide*. He accused her of writing her first memoir, *Looking Back*, published when she was nineteen, in order to become famous. For years after their breakup, Maynard remained silent about their relationship. When she finally decided to write about it, many of Salinger's fans were shocked and angered that Maynard would cash in on the writer's carefully guarded privacy. Many others were terribly curious about what she would say. Fear of legal problems prevented Maynard from publishing any of the couple's letters. And Salinger had never let her see him at work or read any of his writing. Her book focused on her own feelings and experiences.

In 1999, Maynard was once again criticized when she auctioned off the personal letters Salinger had written to her during their romance. The letters were bought by the California software entrepreneur and philanthropist Peter Norton, who returned them to Salinger.

The most recent, and most dramatic, invasion of Salinger's privacy was the publication of Margaret Salinger's autobiographical memoir, *Dream Catcher*, in 2000. Aside from linking Salinger's life to his fiction, the 500-page book revealed many interesting and intimate details about the famous author. Margaret was greeted

The Betty Eppes Story

Betty Eppes was a young reporter from the *Baton Rouge Advocate*. In the spring of 1980, she was a writer for the newspaper's "Fun" section. As an assignment, she decided to spend her summer vacation trying to interview J. D. Salinger. She wrote him a letter in which she described herself as a tall writer with green eyes and red-gold hair who very much wanted to see him. Surprisingly, Salinger agreed to meet with her in Cornish.

During their very brief interview, which Eppes tape-recorded, Salinger admitted to not knowing how or why he became a writer. He also said that he had no plans to publish. In fact, he said that he felt he would have been happier if he had never published at all, that the publishing world was vicious.

At one point, overcome by emotion, Eppes began to cry and Salinger tenderly wiped the tears from her face. Seeing them speaking together, a strange man stopped and put his hand out to touch Salinger in greeting. Salinger flew into a rage and yelled at Eppes that the man's gesture was her fault. Before Salinger stalked off, she sneakily took two pictures of the author, still tall and handsome, with white hair.

with criticism from Salinger fans and from her own brother, Matthew. They accused her of trying to take advantage of her father's name or to get back at him for being, in some ways, an absent and difficult father. Margaret countered that she wrote it to make some sense of her strange childhood and also to end the vow of silence that had always been the strict (if unspoken) rule in the Salinger family. She argued that it was more honest to write about her father while he was alive and could defend himself than to wait until he was dead and publish behind his back. Yet, at the time of the memoir's release, Margaret admitted she and her father hadn't spoken about the book. She was going to give him some time to cool down before getting in touch with him. As she joked to a reporter, "I may be forty-four, but I still don't want to get yelled at."[3]

Interview with J. D. Salinger

The following interview of J. D. Salinger by Lacey Fosburgh was excerpted from an article in the *New York Times*. The interview took place on November 3, 1974.

Goaded by publication of unauthorized editions of his early, previously uncollected works, the reclusive author J. D. Salinger broke a public silence of more than 20 years last week, issuing a denunciation and revealing he is hard at work on writings that may never be published in his lifetime.

Speaking by telephone from Cornish, N. H., where he makes his home, the 55-year-old author whose most recent published work, "Raise High the Roof Beam, Carpenters" and "Seymour, an Introduction," appeared in 1962, said, "There is a marvelous peace in not publishing. It's peaceful. Still. Publishing is a terrible invasion of my privacy. I like to write. I love to write. But I write just for myself and my own pleasure."

For nearly half an hour after saying he intended to talk "only for a minute," the author, who achieved literary fame and cultish devotion enhanced by his inaccessibility following publication of "The Catcher in the Rye" in 1951, spoke of his work, his obsession with privacy and his uncertain thoughts about publication.

The interview with Mr. Salinger, who was at times warm and charming, at times wary and skittish, is believed to be his first since 1953, when he granted one to a 16-year-old representative of the high school newspaper in Cornish.

What prompted Mr. Salinger to speak now on what he said was a cold, rainy, windswept night in Cornish was what he regards as the latest and most severe of all invasions of his private world: the publication of "The Complete Uncollected Short Stories of J. D. Salinger, Vols. 1 and 2."

During the last two months, about 25,000 copies of these books, priced at $3 to $5 for each volume, have been sold—first here in San Francisco, then in New York, Chicago and elsewhere, according to Mr. Salinger, his lawyers and book dealers around the country.

"Some stories, my property, have been stolen," Mr. Salinger said. "Someone's appropriated them. It's an illicit act. It's unfair. Suppose you had a coat you liked and somebody went into your closet and stole it.

That's how I feel."

Mr. Salinger wrote the stories, including two about Holden Caulfield, the pained, sensitive hero of "The Catcher in the Rye," between 1940 and 1948 for magazines like The Saturday Evening Post, Collier's and Esquire.

Prefiguring his later writing, they concern themselves with lonely young soldiers and boys who eat egg yolks, girls with "lovely, awkward" smiles and children who never get letters.

"Selling Like Hotcakes"

"They're selling like hotcakes," said one San Francisco book dealer. "Everybody wants one."

While "The Catcher in the Rye" still sells at the rate of 250,000 copies a year, the contents of the unauthorized paperback books have been available heretofore only in the magazine files of large libraries.

"I wrote them a long time ago," Mr. Salinger said of the stories, "and I never had any intention of publishing them. I wanted them to die a perfectly natural death.

"I'm not trying to hide the gaucheries of my youth. I just don't think they're worthy of publishing."

Since last April, copies of "The Complete Uncollected Short Stories of J. D. Salinger, Vols. 1 and 2" have reportedly been peddled in person to bookstores at $1.50 each by men who always call themselves John Greenberg and say they come from Berkeley, Calif. Their descriptions have varied from city to city.

One such peddler told Andreas Brown, manager of the Gotham Book Mart in New York City, that he and his associates did not expect to get in trouble for their unauthorized enterprise because, as Mr. Brown related, "they could always negotiate with Salinger's lawyers and promise not to do it any more."

Mr. Brown, who described the young man as "a hippie, intellectual type, a typical Berkeley student," said, "I asked him why they were doing it, and he said he was a fan of Salinger's and thought these stories should be available to the public.

"I asked him what he thought Salinger would feel, and he said, 'We thought if we made the books attractive enough he wouldn't mind.'"

Gotham refused to sell the books and alerted Mr. Salinger to the unauthorized publications.

"It's irritating," said Mr. Salinger, who said he still owns the copyright on the stories. "It's really very irritating. I'm very upset about it."

According to Neil L. Shapiro, one of the author's lawyers here, the publication or sale of the stories without Mr. Salinger's authorization violates Federal copyright laws.

A civil suit in Mr. Salinger's name was filed last month in the Federal District Court here against "John Greenberg" and 17 major local bookstores, including Brentano's, alleging violation of the copyright laws.

The author is seeking a minimum of $250,000 in punitive damages and injunctive relief.

The stories have since been enjoined from all further sales of the unauthorized books, and, according to Mr. Shapiro, they still face possible damage payments ranging from $4,500 to

$90,000 for each book sold. Additional legal action, he said, was being planned against bookstores elsewhere.

The mysterious publisher and his associates remain at large.

It's amazing some sort of law and order agency can't do something about this," Mr. Salinger said. "Why, if a dirty old mattress is stolen from your attic, they'll find it. But they're not even looking for this man."

Discusses Opposition

Discussing his opposition to republication of his early works, Mr. Salinger said they were the fruit of a time when he was first beginning to commit himself to being a writer. He spoke of writing feverishly, of being "intent on placing [his works] in magazines."

Suddenly he interrupted himself.

"This doesn't have anything to do with this man Greenberg," he said. "I'm still trying to protect what privacy I have left."

Over the years many newspapers and national magazines have sent their representatives to his farmhouse in Cornish, but the author would turn and walk away if approached on the street and was reported to abandon friends if they discussed him with reporters. There have been articles reporting on his mailbox, his shopping and his reclusive life, but not interviews.

But last week, he responded to a request for an interview transmitted to him earlier in the day, by Dorothy Olding, his New York literary agent.

Did he expect to publish another work soon?

There was a pause.

"I really don't know how soon," he said. There was another pause, and then Mr. Salinger began to talk rapidly about how much he was writing, long hours, every day, and he said he was under contract to no one for another book.

"I don't necessarily intend to publish posthumously," he said, "but I do like to write for myself.

"I pay for this kind of attitude. I'm known as a strange, aloof kind of man. But all I'm doing is trying to protect myself and my work."

"I just want all this to stop. It's intrusive. I've survived a lot of things," he said in what was to be the end of the conversation, "and I'll probably survive this."

Timeline

1919 Jerome David Salinger is born on New Year's Day in New York City.

1932 Salinger is enrolled at McBurney private school, in Manhattan.

1934 Salinger is sent to Valley Forge Military Academy, in Pennsylvania.

1936 Salinger graduates from Valley Forge.

1937 Salinger's father sends him to Vienna and Poland to learn about his business, importing hams and cheeses.

1938 For a few months, Salinger attends Ursinus College in Pennsylvania, where he writes film reviews for the college newspaper.

1939 Salinger takes Whit Burnett's short story writing class at Columbia University, in New York.

1940 Salinger's first published short story, "The Young Folks," appears in Whit Burnett's *Story* magazine. Salinger is paid $25.

1941 The *New Yorker* buys Salinger's first story featuring Holden Caulfield, "Slight Rebellion off Madison." Publication is delayed until 1946, due to the United States entering World War II.

1942 Salinger is drafted into the U.S. Army.

1943 Salinger becomes a sergeant and begins counterintelligence training.

1944 As part of the Twelfth Infantry Regiment, Salinger is one of the first to land on the beaches of Normandy during the D-day operations. He participates in five more European campaigns. He is among the first troops that liberate Paris from the Nazis and one of the first to see the horrors of the German concentration camps.

1945 Discharged from the army, Salinger returns to New York. Among the short stories he publishes is "I'm Crazy," which appears in *Collier's*, and is the first published story to include material used in *The Catcher in the Rye*.

1946 A ninety-page novella about Holden Caulfield is accepted for publication, but is withdrawn by Salinger.

1948 Salinger moves to Westport, Connecticut. He begins his long exclusive association with the distinguished *New Yorker* literary magazine. The *New Yorker* publishes "A Perfect Day for Bananafish," the first to feature Seymour Glass, in which the protagonist blows his head off with a gun. His story "A Girl I Knew" is selected for the Best American Short Stories of 1949.

1950 Salinger begins studying Vedanta, an Eastern philosophy that is an offshoot of Hinduism.

1951 *The Catcher in the Rye* is published.

1953 Salinger moves to Cornish, New Hampshire. He meets Claire Douglas. *Nine Stories* is published.

1955 Salinger and Claire are married in February. In December, their daughter, Margaret, is born. "Franny" and "Raise High the Roof Beam, Carpenters" are published in the *New Yorker*.

1957 "Zooey" is published in the *New Yorker*.

1959 "Seymour—an Introduction" is published in the *New Yorker*.

1960 Salinger and Claire's son, Matthew, is born in February.

1961 *Franny and Zooey* is published.

1963 *Raise High the Roof Beam, Carpenters and Seymour—an Introduction* is published.

1965 Salinger publishes his last story, "Hapworth 16, 1924," in the *New Yorker*.

1967 Salinger and Claire are divorced.

1974 *Complete Uncollected Short Stories* of J. D. Salinger is published, without Salinger's permission, in California. Salinger decides to sue for violation of his privacy.

1986 The suit against California bookstores for selling his *Uncollected Short Stories* is settled in Salinger's favor. Salinger tries to stop publication of an unauthorized biography by British writer Ian Hamilton.

1987 The U.S. Supreme Court rules in Salinger's favor, prohibiting the release of Hamilton's biography.

1998 Writer Joyce Maynard publishes *At Home in the World*, in which she describes for the first time her nine-month relationship with J. D. Salinger.

2000 Salinger's daughter, Margaret, publishes *Dream Catcher: A Memoir*, in which she tells about growing up with her famous father.

List of
Selected Works

The Catcher in the Rye. Boston, MA: Little,
   Brown & Company, 1951.
Franny and Zooey, Boston, MA: Little, Brown
   & Company, 1961.
Nine Stories. Boston, MA: Little, Brown &
   Company, 1953.
*Raise High the Roof Beam, Carpenters and
   Seymour—an Introduction*. Boston, MA:
   Little, Brown & Company, 1963.

List of
Selected Awards

***The Catcher in the Rye* (1951)**
Midsummer selection of the Book-of-the-
Month Club (1951)
Reaches fourth place on the *New York Times*
best-seller list (1951)
Selected as one of twelve Best American
Postwar Novels by the library staff of the
United States Information Service (1963)

"For Esmé—with Love and Squalor" (1950)
Selected for Prize Stories of 1950
Selected as an O. Henry Prize Story (1963)

***Franny and Zooey* (1961)**
Reaches first place on the *New York Times*
best-seller list (1961)

"A Girl I Know" (1948)
Selected for Best American Short Stories
of 1949

Glossary

acupuncture The Chinese method of curing pain or disease by inserting needles into specific parts of the body.

Allies The union of England, France, the United States, Russia, and other nations that fought against Germany, Japan, and Italy during World War II.

anguish Extreme pain, distress, or anxiety.

antihero A complex modern hero with good qualities as well as some of the character flaws traditionally associated with villains.

anti-Semitism Discrimination against or hatred for Jewish people.

Buddhism A religion of eastern and central Asia based on the teachings of the prophet

Buddha that follow the belief that life's sufferings can be overcome by achieving mental and moral purity.

Christian Science The Christian-based church and religion founded by Mary Baker Eddy that focuses on healing through spiritual means.

clique An exclusive group of people who share common views or interests.

conformity An action or behavior in agreement with a socially acceptable set of rules.

controversy A dispute in which strongly held opposite viewpoints come into conflict.

convent A community house of Catholic nuns.

D-day June 6, 1944, the day the Allied forces landed in France during World War II.

denunciation Condemnation, severe criticism, or accusation.

elope To run off and get married in secret.

enlightenment A blessed state of being beyond desire or suffering.

flip Lacking in proper respect or seriousness.

foxhole A pit dug for shelter from enemy gunfire.

gentile Someone who is not Jewish.

Hinduism The main religion of India, the practices and philosophy of which revolve around a belief in reincarnation (life after death) and in a supreme being that guides all living things.

homeopathy The medical practice in which tiny fractions of a disease-causing substance are administered in order to prevent the development of that specific disease.

hypocrite A person who pretends to be good or virtuous in public, but in private acts otherwise.

inconsistency A lack of coherency or logic.

indelible Everlasting, unforgettable.

Ivy League Related to a group of old, private East Coast American universities with high academic reputations and social prestige.

ludicrous Ridiculous.

macrobiotics A grain-based diet influenced by Chinese philosophical ideas.

pathetic Sad, worthy of pity.

philanthropist Someone involved in doing good or charitable works for others.

pirated Reproduced illegally, without permission or copyright.

post-traumatic stress disorder The psychological reaction to a traumatic or horrible event that can include blocking out the event, anxiety, nightmares, and depression.

precursor Someone or something that precedes, comes before, or announces someone or something to come.

preposterous Absurd, incredibly unreasonable.

profane Irreverent; marked by disrespect for something religious or holy.

prose Literary writing that is not poetry.

psychoanalyst A doctor who treats emotional and mental problems by having the patient examine his or her dreams and childhood experiences.

recluse A person who withdraws from the world to live in isolation.

revulsion Extreme disgust.

rye A type of thick grass whose grains are used to make bread or whiskey.

salvation The state of being saved or liberated, usually from sin, destruction, or failure.

Scientology A belief system developed by L. Ron Hubbard in 1955, in which each person is an immortal spiritual being whose survival depends on him or herself and his or her union with others and the universe.

taboo Something prohibited because it shocks or frightens traditional society.

tour-de-force A feat of strength, talent, or genius.

vaudeville An early twentieth-century American form of stage entertainment that mixed theater, stand-up comedy, song, dance, and circus and magic routines.

Yiddish A form of German spoken by Eastern and Central European Jews and written with Hebrew characters.

yoga The Hindu discipline that trains the consciousness to reach a state of perfect peace and spirituality. Also refers to the series of exercises practiced in order to control one's mind and body.

For More Information

Due to the changing nature of Internet links, the Rosen Publishing Group, Inc., has developed an online list of Web sites related to the subject of this book. This site is updated regularly. Please use this link to access the list:

http://www.rosenlinks.com/lab/jdsa

For Further Reading

Alexander, Paul. *Salinger: A Biography*. Los Angeles, CA: Renaissance Books, 1999.

Kotzen, Kip, and Thomas Beller. *With Love and Squalor: 14 Writers Respond to the Work of J. D. Salinger*. New York, NY. Broadway Books, 2001.

Kubica, Chris, and Will Hochman. *Letters to J. D. Salinger*. Madison, WI: University of Wisconsin Press, 2002.

Maynard, Joyce. *At Home in the World*. New York, NY: Picador, 1998.

Salinger, Margaret A. *Dream Catcher: A Memoir*. New York, NY: Washington Square Press, 2000.

Steed, J. P., ed. *The Catcher in the Rye: New Essays*. New York, NY: Peter Lang, 2002.

Bibliography

Bratman, Fred. "Holden, 50, Still Catches."
New York Times, December 21, 1979.
Retrieved August 2000 (http://www.
nytimes.com/books/98/09/13/specials/
salinger-holden.html).

Burger, Nash K. "Books of the Times: The
Catcher in the Rye." Review of *The
Catcher in the Rye. New York Times*, July
16, 1951. Retrieved August 2004 (http://
www.nytimes.com/books/98/09/13/
specials/salinger-rye02.html).

Dougal, Sundeep. "Yet Another Page on J. D.
Salinger?" Retrieved August 2004 (http://
members.tripod.com/~SundeepDougal/
jds.html).

Fosburgh, Lacey. "J. D. Salinger Speaks About His Silence." *New York Times*, November 3, 1974. Retrieved August 2004 (http://www. nytimes.com/books/98/09/13/specials/ salinger-speaks.html).

French, Warren. *J. D. Salinger Revisited*. Boston, MA: Twayne Publishers, 1988.

Goodman, Anne. "Mad About Children." Review of *The Catcher in the Rye*. *New Republic*, Vol. 125, No. 3, July 16, 1951, pp. 20–21.

Hutchens, John K. "On the Books & On an Author: J. D. Salinger." *New York Herald Tribune Book Review*, August 19, 1951.Retrieved August 2004 (http://nths.newtrier.k12.il.us/academics/ english/catcher/NYHTribune.html).

Kakutani, Michiko. "From Salinger, A New Dash of Mystery." *New York Times*, February 20, 1997. Retrieved August 2004 (http://www. nytimes.com/books/98/09/13/specials/ salinger-hapworth.html).

Kegel, Charles. "Incommunicability in Salinger's The Catcher in the Rye" in *Studies in J. D. Salinger: Reviews, Essays, and Critiques of The Catcher in the Rye and Other Fiction*, ed. Marvin Laser. New York, NY: Odyssey Press, 1963, pp. 53–56.

Lomazoff, Eric. *The Praises and Criticisms of J. D. Salinger's The Catcher in the Rye*. 1996.

Retrieved August 2004 (http://www.levity.com/corduroy/salinger1.htm).

Longstreth, T. Morris. "New Novels in the News." Review of *The Catcher in the Rye*. *Christian Science Monitor*, July 19, 1951. Retrieved August 2004 (http://nths.newtrier.k12.il.us/academics/english/catcher/CSMonitor.html).

MacFarquahar, Larissa. "The Cult of Joyce Maynard." *New York Times Magazine*, September 6, 1998. Retrieved August 2004 (http://www.nytimes.com/library/books/090698mag-maynard.html).

McDowell, Edwin. "Publishing: Visit with J. D. Salinger." *New York Times*, September 11, 1981.

Morill, Sarah. "A Brief Biography of J. D. Salinger." April 2002. Retrieved July 2004. (http://www.morrill.org/books/salbio.shtml).

Pollitt, Katha. "With Love and Squalor: Joyce Maynard Recalls Her Brief Affair with J. D. Salinger over 25 Years Ago." *New York Times*, September 13, 1998. Retrieved August 2000 (http://www.nytimes.com/books/98/09/13/reviews/980913.13pollitt.html).

Poore, Charles. "Books of the Times: Nine Stories." *New York Times*, April 9, 1953. Retrieved August 2000 (http://www.nytimes.com/books/98/09/13/specials/salinger-stories02.html).

Prescott, Orville. "Books of the Times: Raise High the Roof Beam, Carpenter and Seymour—an Introduction." *New York Times*, January 28, 1963. Retrieved August 2000 (http://www.nytimes.com/books/98/09/13/specials/salinger-raise.html).

Richler, Mordecai. "Summer Reading; Rises at Dawn, Writes, Then Retires." Review of *In Search of J. D. Salinger*. *New York Times*, June 5, 1988. Retrieved August 2000 (http://www.nytimes.com/books/98/09/13/specials/salinger-search.html).

Romano, John. "Salinger Was Playing Our Song." *New York Times*, June 3, 1979. Retrieved August 2000 (http://www.nytimes.com/books/98/09/13/specials/salinger-song.html).

Salinger, J. D. *The Catcher in the Rye*. Boston, MA: Little, Brown & Company, 1991.

Salinger, J. D. *Franny and Zooey*. New York, NY: Bantam Books, 1969.

Salinger, J. D. "Last Day of the Last Furlough." *Saturday Evening Post*, July 15, 1944.

Salinger, J. D. *Nine Stories*. Boston, MA: Little, Brown & Company, 1991.

Salinger, J. D. *Raise High the Roof Beam, Carpenters and Seymour—an Introduction*. New York, NY: Bantam Books, 1971.

Salinger, Margaret A. *Dream Catcher: A Memoir*. New York, NY: Washington Square Press, 2000.

Smith, Dinitia. "J. D. Salinger to Be Focus of a Memoir." *New York Times*, November 21, 1997. Retrieved August 2004 (http://www. nytimes.com/books/98/09/13/specials/ maynard-salinger.html).

Smith, Dinitia. "Salinger's Daughter's Truths as Mesmerizing as His Fiction." *New York Times*, August 30, 2000. Retrieved August 2004 (http://partners.nytimes.com/library/ books/083000salinger-daughter.html).

Smith, Harrison. "Manhattan Ulysses, Junior." Review of *The Catcher in the Rye*. *Saturday Review of Literature*, July 14, 1951. Retrieved August 2004 (http://nths.newtrier.k12.il.us/ academics/english/catcher/SatReview.html).

Stern, James. "Aw, The World's a Crumby Place." Review of *The Catcher in the Rye*. *New York Times*, July 15, 1951. Retrieved August 2004 (http://www.nytimes.com/ books/98/09/13/specials/salinger-rye01.html).

Updike, John. "Anxious Days for the Glass Family." Review of *Franny and Zooey*. *New York Times*, September 17, 1961. Retrieved August 2004 (http://www.nytimes.com/books/ 98/09/13/specials/salinger-franny01.html).

Welty, Eudora. "Threads of Innocence." Review of *Nine Stories*. *New York Times*, April 5, 1953. Retrieved August 2000 (http://www. nytimes.com/books/98/09/13/specials/ salinger-stories01.html).

"With Love & 20-20 Vision." Review of *The Catcher in the Rye*. *Time*, July 16, 1951, Retrieved August 2004 (http://nths.newtrier. k12.il.us/academics/english/catcher/Time.html).

Source Notes

Introduction

1. Orville Prescott, "Books of the Times: Raise High the Roof Beam, Carpenters and Seymour—an Introduction," *New York Times*, January 28, 1963. Retrieved August 2000 (http://www.nytimes.com/books/98/09/13/specials/salinger-raise.html).

Chapter 3

1. Harrison Smith, "Manhattan Ulysses, Junior." Review of *The Catcher in the Rye*. *Saturday Review of Literature*, July 14, 1951. Retrieved August 2004 (http://nths.newtrier.k12.il.us/academics/english/ catcher/SatReview.html).

2. T. Morris Longstreth, "New Novels in the News," *Christian Science Monitor*, July 19, 1951. Retrieved August 2004 (http://nths.newtrier.k12.il.us/academics/english/catcher/CSMonitor.html).

3. "With Love & 20-20 Vision," Review of *The Catcher in the Rye*. *Time*, July 16, 1951. Retrieved August 2004 (http://nths.newtrier.k12.il.us/academics/english/catcher/Time.html).

4. Nash K. Burger, "Books of the Times: The Catcher in the Rye." Review of *The Catcher in the Rye*. *New York Times*, July 16, 1951. Retrieved August 2004 (http://www.nytimes.com/books/98/09/13/specials/salinger-rye02.html).

5. Anne Goodman, "Mad About Children." Review of *The Catcher in the Rye*. *New Republic*, Vol. 125, No. 3, July 16, 1951, p. 21.

6. James Stern, "Aw, the World's a Crumby Place." Review of *The Catcher in the Rye*. *New York Times*, July 15, 1951. Retrieved August 2004 (http://www.nytimes.com/books/98/09/13/specials/salinger-rye01.html).

7. "With Love & 20-20 Vision."

8. Longstreth.

9. Smith.

10. Burger.

11. Charles Kegel, "Incommunicability in Salinger's The Catcher in the Rye," in *Studies in J. D. Salinger: Reviews, Essays, and Critiques of The Catcher in the Rye and Other Fiction*, ed. Marvin Laser (New York, NY: Odyssey Press, 1963), pp. 51–56.

12. Longstreth.

Chapter 4

1. United States Information Service, "American Top Twelve," cited in Warren French, *J. D. Salinger Revisited* (Boston, MA: Twayne Publishers, 1988), pp. 51–52.

2. "With Love & 20-20 Vision," Review of *The Catcher in the Rye*. *Time*, July 16, 1951. Retrieved August 2004 (http://nths.newtrier.k12.il.us/academics/english/catcher/Time.html).

3. John Updike, "Anxious Days for the Glass Family," Review of *Franny and Zooey*. *New York Times*, September 17, 1961. Retrieved August 2000 (http://www.nytimes.com/books/98/09/13/specials/salinger-franny01.html).

4. Ibid.

5. Updike.

6. Orville Prescott, "Books of the Times: Raise High the Roof Beam, Carpenter and Seymour—an Introduction." *New York Times*, January 28, 1963. Retrieved August 2000 (http://www.nytimes.com/books/98/09/13/specials/salinger-raise.html).

Chapter 5

1. Mary McCarthy, "J. D. Salinger's Closed Circuit." *Harper's Magazine*, October 1962, p. 47.

2. Margaret A. Salinger, *Dream Catcher: A Memoir* (New York, NY: Washington Square Press, 2000), p. 11.

3. Dinitia Smith, "Salinger's Daughter's Truths as Mesmerizing as His Fiction." *New York Times*, August 30, 2000. Retrieved August 2004 (http://partners.nytimes.com/library/books/083000salinger-daughter.html).

Index

107

About the Author

Michael A. Sommers has a degree in literature from McGill University, Montreal and a masters degree in history and civilizations from the École des Hautes Études en Sciences Sociales, Paris. He has worked as an author and journalist for many years and has written more than thirty books of nonfiction for middle school and young adult readers, two of which were included on the Nonfiction Honor List of Voice of Youth Advocates (VOYA).

Photo Credits

Cover © Getty Images, Inc.; p. 2 © Time Life Pictures/Getty Images, Inc.

Designer: Tahara Anderson; Editor: Annie Sommers; Photo Researcher: Hillary Arnold